Copyright © 2024 by John G. Stringer

All rights reserved. No part of this publication may be reproduced, distributed, or transmitted in any form or by any means, including photocopying, recording, or other electronic or mechanical methods, without the prior written permission of the publisher, except in the case of brief quotations embodied in critical reviews and certain other noncommercial uses permitted by copyright law.

For permissions requests, write to the publisher at the address below:

John G. Stringer

Published by: Kings Media Consult

Cover design by Canvas

First Edition: 2024

10 9 8 7 6 5 4 3 2 1

Preface

Welcome to "Dollar and Sense: Practical Advice for Business Owners."

In the vast and ever-evolving landscape of business management, navigating the complexities and challenges can often feel overwhelming. Whether you're a seasoned entrepreneur or just starting your journey as a business owner, the road to success is paved with numerous decisions, strategies, and lessons learned along the way.

This book is designed to serve as your comprehensive guidebook, offering practical advice, valuable insights, and actionable strategies to help you navigate the intricacies of running a successful business. Drawing on my own experiences as an entrepreneur, as well as insights from industry leaders and successful business owners, "Dollar and Sense" covers a diverse range of topics essential for business success.

From strategic planning and financial management to marketing strategies, human resource management, operations management, and beyond, each chapter is packed with valuable information and practical tips to help you overcome challenges, seize opportunities, and achieve your Desired Business Plan.

TABLE OF CONTENT

Preface
Chapter 1: Setting the Foundation: Crafting a Solid Business Plan
Chapter 2: Managing Cash Flow: Strategies for Sustainable Financial Health
Chapter 3: Budgeting Basics: Allocating Resources Wisely
Chapter 4: Financial Forecasting: Planning for Future Growth and Stability
Chapter 5: Pricing Strategies: Maximizing Profit Margins
Chapter 6: Tax Essentials: Navigating the Complexities of Business Taxes
Chapter 7: Debt Management: Leveraging Debt Responsibly
Chapter 8: Investment Decisions: Maximizing Returns and Managing Risks
Chapter 9: Risk Management: Safeguarding Your Business Against Uncertainty
Chapter 10: Financial Analysis: Unveiling Insights for Informed Decision-Making
Chapter 11: Strategic Planning: Charting the Course for Success

Chapter 12: Performance Management: Driving Excellence and Accountability
Chapter 13: Employee Engagement: Fostering a Culture of Commitment and Productivity
Chapter 14: Innovation and Adaptation: Navigating Change in the Business Landscape
Chapter 15: Strategic Partnerships and Collaboration: Leveraging Synergies for Growth
Chapter 16: Risk Management: Safeguarding Business Operations and Assets
Chapter 17: Financial Management: Navigating the Fiscal Landscape for Business Success
Chapter 18: Marketing Strategies: Navigating the Digital Landscape for Business Growth
Chapter 19: Human Resource Management: Cultivating Talent for Business Success
Chapter 20: Operations Management: Optimizing Efficiency and Effectiveness for Business Excellence
Conclusion: Navigating the Business Landscape with Confidence
Acknowledgments

DOLLAR AND SENSE: PRACTICAL ADVICE FOR BUSINESS OWNERS

AUTHOR
JOHN G. STRINGER

Introduction:

Welcome to "Dollars and Sense: Practical Advice for Business Owners," a comprehensive guide designed to equip entrepreneurs and business owners with the knowledge and strategies needed to navigate the intricate world of finance and business management. In the bustling city of New York, where dreams are forged amidst the towering skyscrapers and bustling streets, countless individuals embark on the journey of entrepreneurship each day, driven by a desire to create, innovate, and succeed.

As the founder of a successful business consultancy firm, I've had the privilege of working with a diverse array of entrepreneurs, from tech startups in Silicon Valley to small family-owned businesses in rural towns. Through these experiences, I've witnessed firsthand the challenges and triumphs that accompany the pursuit of business success. From managing cash flow and navigating complex tax regulations to developing effective marketing strategies and fostering a culture of innovation, the road to entrepreneurial success is paved with obstacles and opportunities at every turn.

In this book, we'll delve into a myriad of topics essential to the financial health and prosperity of your business. We'll explore the importance of crafting a solid business plan as the foundation for success and delve into the intricacies of managing cash flow to ensure sustainable growth. We'll discuss the art of budgeting and financial forecasting, empowering you to make informed decisions that propel your business forward.

But our journey doesn't stop there. We'll also tackle complex issues such as debt management, investment strategies, and risk mitigation, providing you with the tools and insights needed to navigate these challenges with confidence. From understanding the nuances of employee compensation and legal considerations to harnessing the power of technology and data analytics, we'll leave no stone unturned in our quest to arm you with the knowledge and resources needed to thrive in today's competitive business landscape.

Throughout this book, you'll encounter real-world case studies and examples that highlight the successes and setbacks of businesses large and small. From the meteoric rise of tech giants like Amazon and Google to the humble beginnings of local mom-and-pop shops, these stories serve as both inspiration and cautionary tales, offering valuable insights into the strategies and practices that drive business success.

Whether you're a seasoned entrepreneur looking to take your business to new heights or a budding startup founder navigating the challenges of entrepreneurship for the first time, "Dollars and Sense" is your indispensable guide to mastering the art of business finance. So let's embark on this journey together, armed with knowledge, determination, and a steadfast commitment to turning your business dreams into reality.

Chapter 1: Setting the Foundation: Crafting a Solid Business Plan

In the bustling metropolis of New York City, amidst the skyscrapers and bustling streets of Manhattan, lies the vibrant heart of entrepreneurship. Here, dreams are forged, ideas are born, and businesses are built from the ground up. But amidst the hustle and bustle of the city that never sleeps, one thing remains constant: the need for a solid foundation upon which to build your business.

In this chapter, we'll delve into the essential elements of crafting a comprehensive business plan that serves as the roadmap for your entrepreneurial journey. From defining your business model and target market to outlining your marketing and financial strategies, a well-crafted business plan is the cornerstone of success for any venture, no matter its size or industry.

1.1 Defining Your Business Model: The Blueprint for Success

At the heart of every successful business lies a clear and concise business model that outlines how the company intends to create, deliver, and capture value. Whether you're launching a tech startup in Silicon Valley or opening a small retail store in the suburbs, defining your business model is the first step towards building a successful venture.

In this section, we'll explore the various types of business models, from traditional models like product sales and service-based businesses to innovative approaches such as subscription-based pricing and platform-based models. Drawing inspiration from successful companies like Airbnb, Uber, and Netflix, we'll examine how these companies have disrupted traditional industries and redefined the way we do business in the digital age.

1.2 Understanding Your Target Market: Identifying Opportunities and Challenges

No matter how revolutionary your product or service may be, it's essential to understand the needs, preferences, and behaviors of your target market. In this section, we'll discuss the importance of market research and customer segmentation in identifying opportunities and addressing challenges in your industry.

From conducting surveys and focus groups to analyzing market trends and competitor analysis, we'll explore the various methods and techniques for gathering valuable insights into your target market. Drawing on real-world examples from companies like Apple, Coca-Cola, and Tesla, we'll illustrate how market research can inform product development, marketing strategies, and customer engagement initiatives, ultimately driving business growth and profitability.

1.3 Outlining Your Marketing Strategy: Reaching Your Audience and Driving Sales

In today's hyper-connected world, a strong marketing strategy is essential for attracting customers, driving sales, and building brand awareness. In this section, we'll discuss the key components of a successful marketing strategy, from defining your unique selling proposition and positioning to selecting the right channels and tactics for reaching your target audience.

Drawing on examples from both B2B and B2C industries, we'll explore the various marketing channels available to businesses today, from digital marketing and social media advertising to traditional channels like print, radio, and television. We'll also discuss the importance of measuring and analyzing the effectiveness of your marketing efforts, using tools like Google Analytics, Facebook Insights, and customer relationship management (CRM) software to track key metrics and optimize your campaigns for maximum impact.

1.4 Financial Projections: Forecasting Revenue, Expenses, and Cash Flow

No business plan is complete without a thorough financial analysis that outlines your revenue projections, expenses, and cash flow forecasts. In this section, we'll discuss the importance of financial projections in guiding decision-making and securing funding for your business.

Drawing on principles of accounting and finance, we'll explore how to create realistic revenue forecasts based on market trends, sales projections, and pricing strategies. We'll also discuss the importance of accurately estimating your expenses, including fixed costs like rent, utilities, and salaries, as well as variable costs like materials, labor, and marketing expenses.

In addition to revenue and expenses, we'll also delve into the importance of cash flow forecasting in ensuring the financial health and sustainability of your business. By accurately projecting your cash inflows and outflows, you can identify potential cash shortages or surpluses and take proactive measures to manage your liquidity and mitigate financial risks.

1.5 Conclusion: Putting It All Together

As we conclude this chapter, it's clear that crafting a solid business plan is the first step towards building a successful and sustainable business. By defining your business model, understanding your target market, outlining your marketing strategy, and projecting your financials, you can create a roadmap for success that guides your entrepreneurial journey and sets the stage for future growth and prosperity.

In the chapters that follow, we'll delve deeper into the intricacies of business finance, exploring topics such as cash flow management, budgeting, pricing strategies, and investment decisions. But for now, take the time to reflect on the insights and strategies presented in this chapter, and begin laying the groundwork for your own entrepreneurial success story.

Chapter 2: Managing Cash Flow: Strategies for Sustainable Financial Health

In the bustling financial district of Wall Street, where fortunes are made and lost in the blink of an eye, one thing reigns supreme: cash flow. For business owners, managing cash flow effectively is essential for ensuring the financial health and sustainability of their ventures. In this chapter, we'll explore the intricacies of cash flow management and discuss strategies for maintaining a healthy cash flow that fuels growth and prosperity.

2.1 Understanding Cash Flow: The Lifeblood of Your Business

Cash flow is the lifeblood of any business, representing the inflow and outflow of cash and cash equivalents over a specific period. In this section, we'll delve into the importance of cash flow management in ensuring the liquidity and solvency of your business.

Drawing on principles of accounting and finance, we'll explore the difference between cash flow and profitability, highlighting the importance of monitoring both metrics to gauge the financial health of your business. We'll also discuss the various components of cash flow, including operating activities, investing activities, and financing activities, and how each impacts your business's overall cash position.

2.2 Cash Flow Forecasting: Anticipating Peaks and Valleys

One of the keys to effective cash flow management is accurate forecasting, which involves predicting your future cash inflows and outflows based on historical data, market trends, and other relevant factors. In this section, we'll discuss the importance of cash flow forecasting in identifying potential cash shortages or surpluses and taking proactive measures to mitigate financial risks.

Drawing on examples from companies like Starbucks, Amazon, and Walmart, we'll explore various techniques and tools for cash flow forecasting, from simple spreadsheet models to sophisticated cash flow management software. We'll also discuss the role of sensitivity analysis and scenario planning in assessing the impact of different variables and assumptions on your cash flow projections, helping you make informed decisions in an uncertain business environment.

2.3 Managing Accounts Receivable: Accelerating Cash Inflows

For many businesses, managing accounts receivable effectively is essential for maintaining a healthy cash flow. In this section, we'll discuss strategies for accelerating cash inflows and reducing the time it takes to collect payments from customers.

Drawing on best practices from companies like Apple, Nike, and Coca-Cola, we'll explore techniques for improving your invoicing process, establishing clear payment terms and conditions, and incentivizing early payments through discounts and incentives. We'll also discuss the importance of monitoring your accounts receivable aging report and taking proactive measures to follow up on overdue payments, minimizing the risk of bad debt and cash flow disruptions.

2.4 Optimizing Accounts Payable: Maximizing Cash Outflows

In addition to managing accounts receivable, optimizing accounts payable is equally important for maintaining a healthy cash flow. In this section, we'll discuss strategies for maximizing cash outflows and preserving working capital through efficient accounts payable management.

Drawing on examples from companies like Walmart, Amazon, and General Electric, we'll explore techniques for negotiating favorable payment terms with suppliers, streamlining the invoice approval process, and taking advantage of early payment discounts and vendor financing programs. We'll also discuss the importance of optimizing your inventory management practices to reduce carrying costs and minimize the risk of stockouts and obsolescence, freeing up cash for other strategic initiatives.

2.5 Conclusion: Mastering Cash Flow Management

As we conclude this chapter, it's clear that effective cash flow management is essential for ensuring the financial health and sustainability of your business. By understanding the principles of cash flow, forecasting future cash flows accurately, and implementing strategies to accelerate cash inflows and optimize cash outflows, you can maintain a healthy cash flow that fuels growth and prosperity.

In the chapters that follow, we'll delve deeper into other aspects of business finance, including budgeting, financial analysis, and investment decisions. But for now, take the time to reflect on the insights and strategies presented in this chapter, and begin implementing them in your own business to master the art of cash flow management.

Chapter 3: Budgeting Basics: Allocating Resources Wisely

In the bustling world of business, where competition is fierce and resources are finite, effective budgeting is essential for success. In this chapter, we'll explore the fundamentals of budgeting and discuss strategies for allocating resources wisely to drive growth and profitability.

3.1 The Importance of Budgeting: A Roadmap for Financial Success

Budgeting is the process of creating a detailed plan that outlines your business's financial goals and objectives, as well as the resources needed to achieve them. In this section, we'll discuss the importance of budgeting in providing a roadmap for financial success and guiding decision-making across all areas of your business.

Drawing on principles of management accounting and financial planning, we'll explore the benefits of budgeting, including improved decision-making, enhanced resource allocation, and greater accountability and control. We'll also discuss the different types of budgets commonly used in business, from static budgets and flexible budgets to zero-based budgets and rolling budgets, and how each can be tailored to meet the unique needs and challenges of your business.

3.2 Creating a Master Budget: Integrating Financial and Operational Plans

A master budget is a comprehensive financial plan that consolidates all of your business's operating and financial budgets into a single document. In this section, we'll discuss the process of creating a master budget and the key components that should be included, such as sales forecasts, production budgets, operating expenses, and capital expenditures.

Drawing on examples from companies like Procter & Gamble, Toyota, and Microsoft, we'll explore techniques for developing accurate sales forecasts based on market trends, historical data, and input from sales teams. We'll also discuss how to create production budgets that align with your sales projections and optimize your manufacturing processes to minimize costs and maximize efficiency.

3.3 Monitoring and Variance Analysis: Tracking Performance Against Targets

Once your master budget is in place, it's essential to monitor your actual performance against your budgeted targets and identify any variances or deviations that may occur. In this section, we'll discuss the importance of monitoring and variance analysis in identifying opportunities for improvement and taking corrective action to stay on track towards your financial goals.

Drawing on principles of managerial accounting and performance management, we'll explore techniques for monitoring key performance indicators (KPIs) and conducting variance analysis to identify the root causes of budget variances. We'll also discuss the importance of communication and collaboration across departments in addressing budgetary issues and implementing corrective actions to mitigate risks and capitalize on opportunities.

3.4 Flexible Budgeting: Adapting to Changing Business Conditions

In today's dynamic business environment, flexibility is essential for success. In this section, we'll discuss the concept of flexible budgeting and how it can help your business adapt to changing market conditions, customer preferences, and competitive pressures.

Drawing on examples from companies like Amazon, Netflix, and Airbnb, we'll explore techniques for creating flexible budgets that can be adjusted quickly and easily in response to changing circumstances. We'll also discuss the importance of scenario planning and sensitivity analysis in evaluating the potential impact of different scenarios on your budget and identifying strategies to mitigate risks and capitalize on opportunities.

3.5 Conclusion: Mastering the Art of Budgeting

As we conclude this chapter, it's clear that effective budgeting is essential for success in today's competitive business landscape. By creating a comprehensive master budget, monitoring performance against targets, and adapting quickly to changing business conditions, you can allocate your resources wisely and drive growth and profitability for your business.

In the chapters that follow, we'll delve deeper into other aspects of business finance, including financial forecasting, investment decisions, and risk management. But for now, take the time to reflect on the insights and strategies presented in this chapter, and begin implementing them in your own business to master the art of budgeting and achieve your financial goals.

Chapter 4: Financial Forecasting: Planning for Future Growth and Stability

In the ever-evolving landscape of business, where change is constant and uncertainty is a fact of life, the ability to forecast future financial performance is essential for success. In this chapter, we'll explore the art and science of financial forecasting and discuss strategies for planning for future growth and stability.

4.1 The Importance of Financial Forecasting: Anticipating Trends and Challenges

Financial forecasting is the process of predicting future financial outcomes based on historical data, market trends, and other relevant factors. In this section, we'll discuss the importance of financial forecasting in helping businesses anticipate trends and challenges, identify opportunities for growth, and make informed strategic decisions.

Drawing on examples from companies like Google, Apple, and Microsoft, we'll explore how financial forecasting can help businesses plan for expansion, allocate resources wisely, and navigate economic downturns and other external shocks. We'll also discuss the different types of financial forecasts commonly used in business, including income statements, balance sheets, and cash flow statements, and how each can provide valuable insights into your business's financial health and performance.

4.2 Techniques for Financial Forecasting: From Simple to Sophisticated

There are many techniques and methods for financial forecasting, ranging from simple extrapolation of historical trends to sophisticated statistical models and machine learning algorithms. In this section, we'll explore some of the most commonly used techniques for financial forecasting and discuss their strengths, limitations, and applications in different business contexts.

Drawing on principles of statistics, econometrics, and data science, we'll explore techniques such as time series analysis, regression analysis, and exponential smoothing, and how they can be used to forecast sales, expenses, and other key financial variables. We'll also discuss the importance of incorporating qualitative factors, such as market research, industry trends, and expert judgment, into your forecasting process to improve accuracy and reliability.

4.3 Scenario Planning: Preparing for the Unexpected

In today's uncertain business environment, scenario planning is becoming increasingly important for businesses looking to mitigate risks and capitalize on opportunities. In this section, we'll discuss the concept of scenario planning and how it can help businesses prepare for the unexpected and adapt to changing circumstances.

Drawing on examples from companies like Amazon, Walmart, and BP, we'll explore techniques for creating and analyzing different scenarios, from best-case to worst-case scenarios, and identifying strategies to mitigate risks and capitalize on opportunities. We'll also discuss the importance of flexibility and agility in scenario planning, and how businesses can use scenario analysis to stress-test their strategies and make informed decisions in an uncertain world.

4.4 Financial Modeling: Building a Blueprint for Success

Financial modeling is the process of creating a mathematical representation of a business's financial performance, usually in the form of a spreadsheet model or software program. In this section, we'll discuss the importance of financial modeling in helping businesses analyze and evaluate different scenarios, assess the impact of strategic decisions, and optimize their financial performance.

Drawing on examples from companies like Tesla, Netflix, and Facebook, we'll explore techniques for building and using financial models to forecast revenue, expenses, and cash flow, and evaluate the financial feasibility of investment projects and strategic initiatives. We'll also discuss best practices for financial modeling, including data integrity, transparency, and sensitivity analysis, and how businesses can use financial models to improve decision-making and drive growth and profitability.

4.5 Conclusion: Harnessing the Power of Financial Forecasting

As we conclude this chapter, it's clear that financial forecasting is an essential tool for businesses looking to plan for future growth and stability. By anticipating trends and challenges, using techniques such as scenario planning and financial modeling, businesses can make informed strategic decisions and position themselves for success in today's dynamic business environment.

In the chapters that follow, we'll delve deeper into other aspects of business finance, including risk management, investment decisions, and financial analysis. But for now, take the time to reflect on the insights and strategies presented in this chapter, and begin implementing them in your own business to harness the power of financial forecasting and achieve your long-term financial goals.

Chapter 5: Pricing Strategies: Maximizing Profit Margins

In the competitive landscape of business, pricing is a critical component of success. A well-crafted pricing strategy can not only maximize profit margins but also position a business strategically within its market. In this chapter, we'll explore various pricing strategies and discuss how business owners can effectively set prices to achieve their financial objectives.

5.1 Understanding Pricing Strategy: Balancing Value and Profitability

Pricing strategy involves more than just setting a price tag; it's about finding the optimal balance between capturing value for your product or service and ensuring profitability for your business. In this section, we'll delve into the fundamentals of pricing strategy and discuss how businesses can use pricing as a strategic tool to achieve their financial goals.

Drawing on principles of microeconomics and marketing, we'll explore different approaches to pricing, including cost-based pricing, value-based pricing, and competition-based pricing. We'll also discuss the importance of understanding customer perceptions of value and how businesses can use pricing to communicate their value proposition effectively to customers.

5.2 Cost-Based Pricing: Ensuring Profitability and Sustainability

Cost-based pricing is a common approach to pricing that involves setting prices based on the costs of production, distribution, and overhead. In this section, we'll discuss the advantages and limitations of cost-based pricing and how businesses can use it to ensure profitability and sustainability in the long term.

Drawing on examples from companies like Walmart, Costco, and McDonald's, we'll explore techniques for calculating and allocating costs, including direct costs, indirect costs, and overhead expenses. We'll also discuss strategies for managing costs effectively and optimizing your cost structure to improve profitability and competitive advantage.

5.3 Value-Based Pricing: Capturing Customer Value

Value-based pricing is a pricing strategy that involves setting prices based on the perceived value of your product or service to the customer. In this section, we'll discuss the principles of value-based pricing and how businesses can use it to capture maximum value for their offerings while maintaining customer satisfaction and loyalty.

Drawing on examples from companies like Apple, Tesla, and Starbucks, we'll explore techniques for identifying and quantifying customer value drivers, such as quality, convenience, and brand reputation. We'll also discuss strategies for communicating value to customers effectively and justifying premium prices through differentiation and innovation.

5.4 Dynamic Pricing: Adapting to Market Conditions

Dynamic pricing is a pricing strategy that involves adjusting prices in real-time based on changes in demand, competition, and other market conditions. In this section, we'll discuss the benefits and challenges of dynamic pricing and how businesses can use it to maximize revenue and profitability in today's fast-paced business environment.

Drawing on examples from industries like e-commerce, travel, and hospitality, we'll explore techniques for implementing dynamic pricing, including demand forecasting, price optimization algorithms, and real-time monitoring of market trends. We'll also discuss the importance of transparency and fairness in dynamic pricing and how businesses can use dynamic pricing to improve customer satisfaction and loyalty.

5.5 Conclusion: Crafting a Winning Pricing Strategy

As we conclude this chapter, it's clear that pricing is a complex and multifaceted aspect of business that requires careful consideration and strategic planning. By understanding the principles of pricing strategy and implementing effective pricing strategies, businesses can maximize profit margins, capture customer value, and achieve their financial objectives.

In the chapters that follow, we'll delve deeper into other aspects of business finance, including investment decisions, risk management, and financial analysis. But for now, take the time to reflect on the insights and strategies presented in this chapter, and begin implementing them in your own business to craft a winning pricing strategy that drives growth and profitability.

Chapter 6: Tax Essentials: Navigating the Complexities of Business Taxes

In the world of business, taxes are an inevitable reality that every entrepreneur must contend with. Understanding the intricacies of business taxes is essential for maintaining compliance, minimizing tax liabilities, and maximizing profitability. In this chapter, we'll explore the essentials of business taxes and discuss strategies for navigating the complexities of the tax landscape.

6.1 The Importance of Tax Compliance: Meeting Legal Obligations

Tax compliance is a critical aspect of business operations, as failing to meet your tax obligations can result in severe penalties and legal consequences. In this section, we'll discuss the importance of tax compliance and the various taxes that businesses are required to pay, including income tax, sales tax, payroll tax, and property tax.

Drawing on examples from businesses around the world, we'll explore the different tax regimes and regulations that businesses must navigate, from the corporate tax rates in the United States to the value-added tax (VAT) systems in Europe and Asia. We'll also discuss the role of tax planning and compliance strategies in minimizing tax liabilities and ensuring that businesses remain in good standing with tax authorities.

6.2 Understanding Business Structures: Choosing the Right Tax Entity

The choice of business structure can have significant implications for tax liability, as different entities are subject to different tax rates and treatment. In this section, we'll discuss the various types of business structures, including sole proprietorships, partnerships, corporations, and limited liability companies (LLCs), and how each is taxed under the law.

Drawing on examples from entrepreneurs like Mark Zuckerberg of Facebook, Jeff Bezos of Amazon, and Elon Musk of Tesla, we'll explore the tax advantages and disadvantages of different business structures and how entrepreneurs can choose the right entity to minimize their tax liabilities and achieve their financial objectives. We'll also discuss the process of entity selection and the factors that entrepreneurs should consider when making this critical decision.

6.3 Tax Planning Strategies: Minimizing Tax Liabilities

Tax planning is the process of organizing your financial affairs in a way that minimizes tax liabilities and maximizes tax benefits. In this section, we'll discuss various tax planning strategies that businesses can use to reduce their tax burdens and optimize their financial positions.

Drawing on examples from tax professionals and financial advisors, we'll explore techniques such as income shifting, expense deferral, tax credits, and deductions, and how businesses can leverage these strategies to lower their taxable income and save money on taxes. We'll also discuss the importance of timing and documentation in tax planning and how businesses can stay abreast of changes in tax laws and regulations to ensure compliance and maximize savings.

6.4 Tax Reporting and Compliance: Meeting Filing Deadlines

Tax reporting and compliance are essential aspects of business operations, as businesses are required to file various tax returns and reports with tax authorities on a regular basis. In this section, we'll discuss the process of tax reporting and compliance, including the forms and documents that businesses are required to submit and the deadlines for filing them.

Drawing on examples from tax professionals and accountants, we'll explore best practices for tax record-keeping, documentation, and reporting, and how businesses can streamline their tax compliance processes to avoid penalties and fines. We'll also discuss the role of tax software and technology in simplifying tax reporting and compliance and how businesses can leverage these tools to stay organized and efficient.

6.5 Conclusion: Navigating the Tax Landscape

As we conclude this chapter, it's clear that navigating the complexities of business taxes requires careful planning, compliance, and strategic decision-making. By understanding the essentials of tax compliance, choosing the right business structure, implementing tax planning strategies, and maintaining diligent tax reporting and compliance, businesses can minimize tax liabilities and maximize profitability.

In the chapters that follow, we'll delve deeper into other aspects of business finance, including investment decisions, risk management, and financial analysis. But for now, take the time to reflect on the insights and strategies presented in this chapter, and begin implementing them in your own business to navigate the tax landscape and achieve your financial goals.

Chapter 7: Debt Management: Leveraging Debt Responsibly

In the world of business, debt can be a double-edged sword. When used wisely, it can fuel growth and expansion, but when mismanaged, it can lead to financial distress and insolvency. In this chapter, we'll explore the essentials of debt management and discuss strategies for leveraging debt responsibly to achieve your business objectives.

7.1 Understanding Business Debt: Types and Sources

Business debt comes in many forms, from bank loans and lines of credit to bonds and commercial paper. In this section, we'll discuss the various types and sources of business debt and how each can be used to finance different aspects of your business operations.

Drawing on examples from companies like Apple, Google, and General Electric, we'll explore the advantages and disadvantages of different types of debt financing, including short-term debt, long-term debt, and convertible debt. We'll also discuss the role of debt covenants and collateral in securing debt financing and the importance of understanding the terms and conditions of your debt agreements before signing on the dotted line.

7.2 Debt vs. Equity Financing: Choosing the Right Mix

Debt and equity are two primary sources of financing for businesses, each with its own advantages and drawbacks. In this section, we'll discuss the differences between debt and equity financing and how businesses can choose the right mix of financing to meet their capital needs and risk tolerance.

Drawing on examples from entrepreneurs like Warren Buffett, Mark Cuban, and Richard

Branson, we'll explore the pros and cons of debt financing, including the tax advantages, fixed interest rates, and potential for leverage. We'll also discuss the benefits and drawbacks of equity financing, including the dilution of ownership, loss of control, and potential for conflicts with investors.

7.3 Debt Management Strategies: Minimizing Costs and Risks

Effective debt management involves more than just borrowing money; it's about minimizing costs and risks while maximizing the benefits of debt financing. In this section, we'll discuss strategies for managing debt effectively, including debt consolidation, refinancing, and restructuring.

Drawing on examples from companies like Ford, General Motors, and IBM, we'll explore techniques for reducing interest expenses, extending debt maturities, and negotiating favorable terms with creditors. We'll also discuss the importance of maintaining a healthy debt-to-equity ratio and avoiding excessive leverage that can strain your business's financial resources and jeopardize its long-term viability.

7.4 Debt Repayment: Meeting Obligations and Preserving Cash Flow

Debt repayment is a critical aspect of debt management, as failing to meet your debt obligations can lead to default, bankruptcy, and other serious consequences. In this section, we'll discuss strategies for managing debt repayment effectively and preserving cash flow while meeting your financial commitments.

Drawing on examples from companies like Microsoft, Amazon, and Walmart, we'll explore techniques for prioritizing debt payments, negotiating with creditors, and restructuring debt agreements to improve repayment terms. We'll also discuss the importance of cash flow forecasting and liquidity management in ensuring that your business has the resources it needs to meet its debt obligations and maintain financial stability.

7.5 Conclusion: Harnessing the Power of Debt

As we conclude this chapter, it's clear that debt can be a powerful tool for financing growth and expansion, but it must be managed responsibly to avoid financial pitfalls. By understanding the essentials of debt management, choosing the right mix of financing, and implementing strategies to minimize costs and risks, businesses can leverage debt effectively to achieve their business objectives and drive long-term success.

In the chapters that follow, we'll delve deeper into other aspects of business finance, including investment decisions, risk management, and financial analysis. But for now, take the time to reflect on the insights and strategies presented in this chapter, and begin implementing them in your own business to harness the power of debt and achieve your financial goals.

Chapter 8: Investment Decisions: Maximizing Returns and Managing Risks

Investment decisions are crucial for businesses, as they determine how resources are allocated and can have a significant impact on the company's long-term success. In this chapter, we'll explore the principles of investment decision-making and discuss strategies for maximizing returns while managing risks.

8.1 Understanding Investment Decisions: Evaluating Opportunities

Investment decisions involve assessing various opportunities to allocate resources in ways that generate returns for the business. In this section, we'll discuss the fundamentals of investment decision-making and the criteria used to evaluate investment opportunities.

Drawing on examples from investors like Warren Buffett, Peter Lynch, and Ray Dalio, we'll explore concepts such as risk and return, time value of money, and opportunity cost, and how they influence investment decisions. We'll also discuss the importance of aligning investment decisions with the company's strategic objectives and financial goals to ensure that resources are allocated effectively and efficiently.

8.2 Capital Budgeting: Evaluating Long-Term Investments

Capital budgeting is the process of evaluating long-term investment opportunities, such as new projects, acquisitions, and capital expenditures, to determine their feasibility and potential returns. In this section, we'll discuss the techniques and methods used in capital budgeting and how businesses can use them to make informed investment decisions.

Drawing on examples from companies like Google, Amazon, and ExxonMobil, we'll explore techniques such as net present value (NPV), internal rate of return (IRR), and payback period analysis, and how they can be used to assess the profitability and riskiness of investment projects. We'll also discuss the importance of incorporating qualitative factors, such as strategic fit and market conditions, into the capital budgeting process to ensure that investment decisions are aligned with the company's overall objectives.

8.3 Risk Management: Mitigating Investment Risks

Every investment carries inherent risks, from market volatility and economic uncertainty to operational challenges and regulatory changes. In this section, we'll discuss the principles of risk management and how businesses can use risk management techniques to mitigate investment risks and protect their financial interests.

Drawing on examples from risk management experts and industry leaders, we'll explore techniques such as diversification, hedging, and insurance, and how they can be used to reduce the impact of adverse events and unexpected losses. We'll also discuss the importance of scenario planning and stress testing in assessing the potential impact of different risk scenarios on investment portfolios and developing contingency plans to address them.

8.4 Portfolio Management: Optimizing Investment Portfolios

Portfolio management involves managing a collection of investments, or portfolio, in a way that maximizes returns while minimizing risks. In this section, we'll discuss the principles of portfolio management and how businesses can use portfolio management techniques to optimize their investment portfolios and achieve their financial objectives.

Drawing on examples from portfolio managers and investment analysts, we'll explore techniques such as asset allocation, diversification, and rebalancing, and how they can be used to construct and manage investment portfolios that are aligned with the company's risk tolerance and return expectations. We'll also discuss the importance of monitoring and evaluating portfolio performance regularly and making adjustments as needed to ensure that investment objectives are met.

8.5 Conclusion: Making Informed Investment Decisions

As we conclude this chapter, it's clear that investment decisions are critical for businesses looking to achieve their financial objectives and drive long-term success. By understanding the principles of investment decision-making, evaluating opportunities effectively, managing risks prudently, and optimizing investment portfolios, businesses can make informed investment decisions that create value and generate returns for shareholders.

In the chapters that follow, we'll delve deeper into other aspects of business finance, including risk management, financial analysis, and strategic planning. But for now, take the time to reflect on the insights and strategies presented in this chapter, and begin implementing them in your own business to maximize returns and manage risks effectively in your investment decisions.

Chapter 9: Risk Management: Safeguarding Your Business Against Uncertainty

In the dynamic world of business, uncertainty and risk are ever-present realities that can have significant implications for a company's success. Effective risk management is essential for safeguarding against potential threats and capitalizing on opportunities. In this chapter, we'll explore the principles of risk management and discuss strategies for identifying, assessing, and mitigating risks in your business operations.

9.1 Understanding Risk: Types and Sources

Risk comes in many forms, from financial risks like market volatility and credit default to operational risks like supply chain disruptions and cybersecurity threats. In this section, we'll discuss the different types and sources of risk that businesses face and how they can impact the company's performance and profitability.

Drawing on examples from businesses around the world, we'll explore concepts such as systematic risk and unsystematic risk, and how they influence the overall risk profile of a company. We'll also discuss the importance of risk identification and assessment in understanding the potential impact of different risks on your business operations and financial performance.

9.2 Risk Assessment: Evaluating Probability and Impact

Risk assessment is the process of evaluating the likelihood and consequences of different risks to determine their significance and prioritize them for mitigation. In this section, we'll discuss techniques and methods for risk assessment and how businesses can use them to identify and prioritize risks effectively.

Drawing on examples from risk management professionals and industry experts, we'll explore techniques such as risk matrix analysis, scenario planning, and Monte Carlo simulation, and how they can be used to quantify the probability and impact of different risks on your business operations. We'll also discuss the importance of considering both qualitative and quantitative factors in risk assessment and how businesses can use risk assessment to inform decision-making and resource allocation.

9.3 Risk Mitigation Strategies: Minimizing Impact

Once risks have been identified and assessed, the next step is to develop and implement strategies for mitigating them and reducing their potential impact on your business. In this section, we'll discuss various risk mitigation strategies and how businesses can use them to protect against potential threats and vulnerabilities.

Drawing on examples from companies like Toyota, JPMorgan Chase, and Target, we'll explore techniques such as risk avoidance, risk transfer, risk reduction, and risk acceptance, and how they can be applied to different types of risks across various business functions. We'll also discuss the importance of developing contingency plans and crisis management protocols to respond effectively to unexpected events and minimize their impact on your business operations.

9.4 Insurance and Risk Transfer: Protecting Your Assets

Insurance is a valuable tool for businesses looking to transfer risk to third-party insurers and protect their assets against potential losses. In this section, we'll discuss the principles of insurance and risk transfer and how businesses can use insurance products to mitigate risks and safeguard their financial interests.

Drawing on examples from insurance providers and risk management consultants, we'll explore different types of insurance coverage, including property insurance, liability insurance, and business interruption insurance, and how they can help businesses manage various risks. We'll also discuss the importance of reviewing and updating your insurance coverage regularly to ensure that it remains aligned with your business's evolving risk profile and financial objectives.

9.5 Conclusion: Embracing Risk Management

As we conclude this chapter, it's clear that effective risk management is essential for safeguarding your business against uncertainty and maximizing its long-term success. By understanding the principles of risk management, identifying and assessing risks effectively, and implementing strategies for mitigating them, businesses can protect their assets, capitalize on opportunities, and achieve their financial objectives.

In the chapters that follow, we'll delve deeper into other aspects of business finance, including financial analysis, strategic planning, and performance management. But for now, take the time to reflect on the insights and strategies presented in this chapter, and begin implementing them in your own business to embrace risk management and safeguard your business against uncertainty.

Chapter 10: Financial Analysis: Unveiling Insights for Informed Decision-Making

Financial analysis is a cornerstone of business management, providing valuable insights into a company's performance, profitability, and financial health. In this chapter, we'll delve into the principles of financial analysis and discuss techniques for interpreting financial statements, ratios, and metrics to inform strategic decision-making.

10.1 Understanding Financial Statements: The Language of Business

Financial statements, including the balance sheet, income statement, and cash flow statement, provide a snapshot of a company's financial position, performance, and cash flows. In this section, we'll discuss the components of financial statements and how businesses can use them to assess their financial health and performance.

Drawing on examples from companies like Coca-Cola, Walmart, and Microsoft, we'll explore how to analyze financial statements to evaluate profitability, liquidity, solvency, and efficiency. We'll also discuss common financial statement analysis techniques, such as trend analysis, horizontal and vertical analysis, and ratio analysis, and how they can be used to identify trends, strengths, and weaknesses in a company's financial performance.

10.2 Ratio Analysis: Assessing Performance and Efficiency

Ratio analysis is a powerful tool for evaluating a company's financial performance and efficiency by comparing different financial metrics and ratios. In this section, we'll discuss key financial ratios and how businesses can use them to assess profitability, liquidity, solvency, and operational efficiency.

Drawing on examples from financial analysts and investment professionals, we'll explore common financial ratios such as profitability ratios (e.g., return on equity, gross margin), liquidity ratios (e.g., current ratio, quick ratio), solvency ratios (e.g., debt-to-equity ratio, interest coverage ratio), and efficiency ratios (e.g., inventory turnover, receivables turnover). We'll also discuss how to interpret these ratios in the context of industry benchmarks, historical trends, and peer comparisons to gain insights into a company's financial performance and competitiveness.

10.3 Cash Flow Analysis: Assessing Liquidity and Sustainability

Cash flow analysis is essential for assessing a company's ability to generate cash from its operating activities, invest in growth opportunities, and meet its financial obligations. In this section, we'll discuss the components of the cash flow statement and how businesses can use cash flow analysis to evaluate liquidity, sustainability, and financial flexibility.

Drawing on examples from cash flow statements of companies like Amazon, Apple, and Berkshire Hathaway, we'll explore techniques for analyzing operating cash flow, investing cash flow, and financing cash flow, and how changes in these components can impact a company's overall cash position. We'll also discuss the importance of free cash flow, cash flow ratios, and cash flow forecasting in assessing a company's ability to generate cash and sustain its operations over the long term.

10.4 Financial Forecasting: Planning for the Future

Financial forecasting is the process of predicting future financial outcomes based on historical data, market trends, and other relevant factors. In this section, we'll discuss techniques for financial forecasting and how businesses can use them to plan for future growth, investment, and financing needs.

Drawing on examples from financial analysts and corporate finance professionals, we'll explore techniques such as trend analysis, regression analysis, and scenario planning, and how they can be used to forecast sales, expenses, and cash flows. We'll also discuss the importance of sensitivity analysis and stress testing in evaluating the potential impact of different scenarios on a company's financial performance and developing contingency plans to mitigate risks.

10.5 Conclusion: Leveraging Financial Analysis for Success

As we conclude this chapter, it's clear that financial analysis is a powerful tool for businesses looking to make informed decisions and achieve their financial objectives. By understanding the principles of financial analysis, interpreting financial statements and ratios effectively, and using financial forecasting techniques to plan for the future, businesses can gain valuable insights into their financial performance and position themselves for success in today's competitive business landscape.

In the chapters that follow, we'll delve deeper into other aspects of business finance, including strategic planning, performance management, and investment decisions. But for now, take the time to reflect on the insights and strategies presented in this chapter, and begin implementing them in your own business to leverage financial analysis for success.

Chapter 11: Strategic Planning: Charting the Course for Success

Strategic planning is a foundational process for businesses, guiding decisions and actions to achieve long-term objectives. In this chapter, we'll explore the principles of strategic planning and discuss strategies for developing and implementing effective strategic plans that drive business success.

11.1 Understanding Strategic Planning: Setting the Vision

Strategic planning involves setting a clear vision for the future of the business and developing a roadmap to achieve that vision. In this section, we'll discuss the fundamentals of strategic planning and how businesses can use it to align their resources and activities with their long-term goals and objectives.

Drawing on examples from companies like Amazon, Google, and Apple, we'll explore the components of a strategic plan, including mission statements, vision statements, goals, objectives, and action plans. We'll also discuss the importance of environmental scanning and SWOT analysis in assessing internal strengths and weaknesses and external opportunities and threats to inform strategic decision-making.

11.2 Setting Strategic Objectives: Defining Success

Strategic objectives are specific, measurable goals that businesses aim to achieve within a defined time frame to realize their vision and mission. In this section, we'll discuss techniques for setting strategic objectives and how businesses can use them to drive performance and accountability throughout the organization.

Drawing on examples from business leaders like Jeff Bezos of Amazon, Tim Cook of Apple, and Satya Nadella of Microsoft, we'll explore techniques such as SMART criteria (Specific, Measurable, Achievable, Relevant, Time-bound) and OKRs (Objectives and Key Results) and how they can be used to set clear, actionable objectives that align with the company's strategic priorities. We'll also discuss the importance of cascading objectives throughout the organization and aligning individual goals with corporate objectives to ensure alignment and accountability.

11.3 Strategic Analysis: Assessing Competitive Position

Strategic analysis involves assessing the competitive landscape and identifying opportunities and threats to inform strategic decision-making. In this section, we'll discuss techniques for strategic analysis and how businesses can use them to understand their competitive position and develop strategies for sustainable competitive advantage.

Drawing on examples from industry analysts and competitive intelligence experts, we'll explore techniques such as Porter's Five Forces analysis, SWOT analysis, and PESTLE analysis, and how they can be used to assess industry dynamics, competitive threats, and market opportunities. We'll also discuss the importance of benchmarking and competitor analysis in understanding industry trends and best practices and how businesses can use strategic analysis to identify strategic gaps and develop plans to address them.

11.4 Strategy Formulation: Developing Action Plans

Strategy formulation involves developing action plans and initiatives to achieve strategic objectives and realize the company's vision and mission. In this section, we'll discuss techniques for strategy formulation and how businesses can use them to translate strategic goals into actionable plans and initiatives.

Drawing on examples from strategic planners and business consultants, we'll explore techniques such as the Ansoff Matrix, the BCG Matrix, and the GE-McKinsey Matrix, and how they can be used to identify growth opportunities, allocate resources, and prioritize strategic initiatives. We'll also discuss the importance of strategic alignment and integration in ensuring that strategy formulation is consistent with the company's overall vision, mission, and values.

11.5 Strategy Implementation: Executing the Plan

Strategy implementation involves executing the strategic plan and monitoring progress toward achieving strategic objectives. In this section, we'll discuss techniques for strategy implementation and how businesses can use them to overcome challenges and ensure successful execution of their strategic initiatives.

Drawing on examples from project management professionals and change management experts, we'll explore techniques such as project planning, resource allocation, and performance monitoring, and how they can be used to drive execution and accountability throughout the organization. We'll also discuss the importance of communication and leadership in fostering a culture of strategic execution and ensuring that employees are aligned and engaged in achieving the company's strategic objectives.

11.6 Conclusion: Achieving Business Excellence Through Strategic Planning

As we conclude this chapter, it's clear that strategic planning is essential for businesses looking to achieve long-term success and competitive advantage. By understanding the principles of strategic planning, setting clear objectives, conducting strategic analysis, formulating actionable strategies, and executing the plan effectively, businesses can chart a course for success and achieve their business objectives.

In the chapters that follow, we'll delve deeper into other aspects of business finance, including performance management, organizational development, and leadership. But for now, take the time to reflect on the insights and strategies presented in this chapter, and begin implementing them in your own business to achieve business excellence through strategic planning.

Chapter 12: Performance Management: Driving Excellence and Accountability

Performance management is essential for businesses to monitor, evaluate, and improve the performance of their employees, teams, and operations. In this chapter, we'll explore the principles of performance management and discuss strategies for driving excellence and accountability throughout the organization.

12.1 Understanding Performance Management: A Holistic Approach

Performance management is a comprehensive process that involves setting clear expectations, monitoring performance, providing feedback, and rewarding achievement. In this section, we'll discuss the fundamentals of performance management and how businesses can use it to align individual and organizational goals and drive performance excellence.

Drawing on examples from companies like Google, General Electric, and Toyota, we'll explore the components of performance management, including goal setting, performance appraisal, coaching and development, and rewards and recognition. We'll also discuss the importance of continuous feedback and communication in performance management and how businesses can create a culture of accountability and high performance.

12.2 Setting Performance Goals: SMART Objectives

Setting clear and specific performance goals is the first step in effective performance management. In this section, we'll discuss techniques for setting SMART (Specific, Measurable, Achievable, Relevant, Time-bound) performance objectives and how businesses can use them to align individual goals with organizational priorities and expectations.

Drawing on examples from performance management experts and human resource professionals, we'll explore techniques for setting performance goals that are meaningful, achievable, and aligned with the company's strategic objectives. We'll also discuss the importance of cascading goals throughout the organization and ensuring that individual goals are linked to departmental and corporate goals to drive alignment and accountability.

12.3 Monitoring Performance: Data-Driven Insights

Monitoring performance involves collecting and analyzing data to track progress toward achieving performance goals and objectives. In this section, we'll discuss techniques for monitoring performance effectively and how businesses can use data-driven insights to identify trends, diagnose problems, and make informed decisions.

Drawing on examples from companies like Netflix, Salesforce, and Procter & Gamble, we'll explore techniques for performance measurement, including key performance indicators (KPIs), dashboards, and scorecards, and how they can be used to monitor performance across different dimensions of the business. We'll also discuss the importance of real-time monitoring and continuous feedback in identifying performance gaps and opportunities for improvement and how businesses can use performance data to drive decision-making and resource allocation.

12.4 Providing Feedback and Coaching: Empowering Employees

Providing regular feedback and coaching is essential for helping employees understand their performance expectations, identify areas for improvement, and develop their skills and capabilities. In this section, we'll discuss techniques for providing effective feedback and coaching and how businesses can use them to empower employees and drive performance improvement.

Drawing on examples from leadership experts and management consultants, we'll explore techniques for giving constructive feedback, conducting performance reviews, and providing coaching and mentoring to support employee development. We'll also discuss the importance of creating a culture of continuous learning and improvement and how businesses can foster open communication and trust to facilitate feedback and coaching interactions.

12.5 Rewarding and Recognizing Achievement: Motivating Excellence

Rewarding and recognizing achievement is essential for motivating employees, fostering engagement, and reinforcing desired behaviors and outcomes. In this section, we'll discuss techniques for rewarding and recognizing performance and how businesses can use them to create a culture of excellence and accountability.

Drawing on examples from companies like Zappos, Southwest Airlines, and Starbucks, we'll explore techniques for designing and implementing effective reward and recognition programs, including monetary incentives, non-monetary rewards, and social recognition. We'll also discuss the importance of fairness and transparency in reward systems and how businesses can use rewards and recognition to reinforce values and behaviors that contribute to organizational success.

12.6 Conclusion: Driving Excellence Through Performance Management

As we conclude this chapter, it's clear that performance management is essential for businesses looking to achieve excellence and drive success. By understanding the principles of performance management, setting clear goals and expectations, monitoring performance effectively, providing feedback and coaching, and rewarding and recognizing achievement, businesses can create a culture of accountability, engagement, and high performance.

In the chapters that follow, we'll delve deeper into other aspects of business management, including organizational development, leadership, and employee engagement. But for now, take the time to reflect on the insights and strategies presented in this chapter, and begin implementing them in your own business to drive excellence through performance management.

Chapter 13: Employee Engagement: Fostering a Culture of Commitment and Productivity

Employee engagement is critical for businesses to cultivate a workforce that is committed, motivated, and productive. In this chapter, we'll explore the principles of employee engagement and discuss strategies for creating a positive work environment where employees feel valued, empowered, and motivated to contribute to the success of the organization.

13.1 Understanding Employee Engagement: The Power of Connection

Employee engagement refers to the emotional commitment and investment that employees have in their work and the organization. In this section, we'll discuss the fundamentals of employee engagement and how businesses can foster a culture of engagement to drive performance and retention.

Drawing on examples from companies like Google, Facebook, and Netflix, we'll explore the components of employee engagement, including job satisfaction, organizational commitment, and discretionary effort. We'll also discuss the importance of communication, collaboration, and trust in building strong relationships between employees and the organization and how businesses can create opportunities for meaningful work and career development to enhance employee engagement.

13.2 Measuring Employee Engagement: The Employee Experience

Measuring employee engagement is essential for understanding the factors that drive engagement and identifying areas for improvement. In this section, we'll discuss techniques for measuring employee engagement and how businesses can use employee feedback to enhance the employee experience.

Drawing on examples from employee engagement surveys and feedback mechanisms used by companies like Airbnb, LinkedIn, and Tesla, we'll explore techniques for measuring employee engagement, including surveys, focus groups, and one-on-one interviews. We'll also discuss the importance of anonymity, confidentiality, and transparency in collecting and analyzing employee feedback and how businesses can use employee engagement data to identify trends, strengths, and opportunities for improvement in the workplace.

13.3 Enhancing Employee Engagement: Creating a Positive Work Environment

Creating a positive work environment is essential for fostering employee engagement and satisfaction. In this section, we'll discuss strategies for enhancing employee engagement and creating a workplace culture where employees feel valued, respected, and motivated to perform at their best.

Drawing on examples from companies known for their strong workplace cultures, such as Patagonia, Southwest Airlines, and HubSpot, we'll explore strategies for enhancing employee engagement, including fostering open communication, promoting work-life balance, and recognizing and rewarding employee contributions. We'll also discuss the importance of leadership and management practices in creating a supportive and inclusive work environment where employees feel empowered to voice their opinions, share ideas, and take ownership of their work.

13.4 Empowering Employee Development: Investing in Growth

Investing in employee development is essential for fostering engagement and retention and building a skilled and motivated workforce. In this section, we'll discuss strategies for empowering employee development and creating opportunities for learning, growth, and advancement within the organization.

Drawing on examples from companies like IBM, Salesforce, and Microsoft, we'll explore techniques for employee development, including training programs, mentorship opportunities, and tuition reimbursement. We'll also discuss the importance of career planning and succession management in helping employees identify their career goals and chart a path for growth and advancement within the organization.

13.5 Sustaining Employee Engagement: Continuous Improvement

Sustaining employee engagement requires ongoing effort and commitment from the organization. In this section, we'll discuss strategies for sustaining employee engagement and fostering a culture of continuous improvement and innovation.

Drawing on examples from companies like Amazon, Intel, and Toyota, we'll explore techniques for sustaining employee engagement, including regular communication and feedback, performance recognition programs, and employee involvement in decision-making processes. We'll also discuss the importance of monitoring employee engagement metrics and trends over time and making adjustments to organizational practices and policies to address changing needs and preferences of employees.

13.6 Conclusion: Cultivating a Culture of Engagement

As we conclude this chapter, it's clear that employee engagement is essential for businesses looking to build a high-performing and motivated workforce. By understanding the principles of employee engagement, measuring engagement effectively, enhancing the employee experience, empowering employee development, and sustaining engagement through continuous improvement, businesses can create a culture where employees are engaged, committed, and passionate about their work and the success of the organization.

In the chapters that follow, we'll delve deeper into other aspects of business management, including leadership, organizational culture, and talent management. But for now, take the time to reflect on the insights and strategies presented in this chapter, and begin implementing them in your own business to cultivate a culture of engagement and drive success through your most valuable asset – your employees.

Chapter 14: Innovation and Adaptation: Navigating Change in the Business Landscape

Innovation and adaptation are critical for businesses to thrive in today's rapidly evolving business landscape. In this chapter, we'll explore the principles of innovation and adaptation and discuss strategies for fostering a culture of creativity, agility, and resilience to navigate change and drive growth.

14.1 Understanding Innovation: The Engine of Growth

Innovation is the process of generating new ideas, products, services, or processes that create value for customers and drive growth for the organization. In this section, we'll discuss the fundamentals of innovation and how businesses can foster a culture of innovation to stay competitive in the marketplace.

Drawing on examples from innovative companies like Tesla, Apple, and Airbnb, we'll explore the components of innovation, including creativity, experimentation, and risk-taking. We'll also discuss the importance of leadership support, cross-functional collaboration, and customer-centricity in fostering innovation and driving continuous improvement and breakthroughs.

14.2 Types of Innovation: From Incremental to Disruptive

Innovation can take many forms, from incremental improvements to existing products or processes to disruptive innovations that fundamentally change industries and markets. In this section, we'll discuss the different types of innovation and how businesses can leverage them to drive growth and competitive advantage.

Drawing on examples from companies like Google, Netflix, and Uber, we'll explore different types of innovation, including product innovation, process innovation, business model innovation, and disruptive innovation. We'll also discuss the importance of understanding market trends, customer needs, and competitive dynamics in identifying opportunities for innovation and developing strategies to capitalize on them.

14.3 The Innovation Process: From Idea to Impact

The innovation process involves a series of steps, from idea generation and validation to implementation and commercialization. In this section, we'll discuss the stages of the innovation process and how businesses can manage innovation effectively to maximize its impact and success.

Drawing on examples from innovation frameworks like Design Thinking, Lean Startup, and Agile methodologies, we'll explore techniques for idea generation, prototyping, testing, and scaling. We'll also discuss the importance of iteration, feedback, and iteration in the innovation process and how businesses can create an environment that fosters experimentation and learning to drive innovation and adaptation.

14.4 Managing Change: Adapting to Market Dynamics

Change is inevitable in the business world, driven by factors such as technological advancements, market disruptions, and shifting consumer preferences. In this section, we'll discuss strategies for managing change effectively and adapting to market dynamics to stay relevant and competitive.

Drawing on examples from companies that have successfully navigated change, such as Amazon, Microsoft, and Starbucks, we'll explore techniques for change management, including communication, stakeholder engagement, and organizational resilience. We'll also discuss the importance of agility, flexibility, and adaptability in responding to change and how businesses can build capabilities and processes that enable them to anticipate and respond to market shifts effectively.

14.5 Building a Culture of Innovation and Adaptation

Building a culture of innovation and adaptation is essential for embedding innovation into the DNA of the organization and driving sustained growth and success. In this section, we'll discuss strategies for building a culture of innovation and adaptation and fostering an environment where creativity, experimentation, and learning are encouraged and celebrated.

Drawing on examples from companies like Google X, 3M, and IDEO, we'll explore techniques for fostering a culture of innovation, including leadership support, employee empowerment, and reward and recognition systems. We'll also discuss the importance of diversity, inclusion, and psychological safety in fostering creativity and collaboration and how businesses can create structures and processes that support innovation and adaptation at all levels of the organization.

14.6 Conclusion: Embracing Innovation and Adaptation

As we conclude this chapter, it's clear that innovation and adaptation are essential for businesses looking to thrive in today's dynamic business landscape. By understanding the principles of innovation, managing change effectively, and building a culture of creativity and agility, businesses can position themselves for long-term success and growth in an ever-changing world.

In the chapters that follow, we'll delve deeper into other aspects of business management, including strategic planning, leadership, and talent management. But for now, take the time to reflect on the insights and strategies presented in this chapter, and begin implementing them in your own business to embrace innovation and adaptation and drive success in today's competitive business environment.

Chapter 15: Strategic Partnerships and Collaboration: Leveraging Synergies for Growth

Strategic partnerships and collaboration play a crucial role in the success and growth of businesses, enabling them to access new markets, technologies, and resources while leveraging synergies and shared expertise. In this chapter, we'll explore the principles of strategic partnerships and collaboration and discuss strategies for establishing and managing successful partnerships to drive business growth.

15.1 Understanding Strategic Partnerships: Creating Value through Collaboration

Strategic partnerships involve formal agreements between two or more organizations to collaborate on specific projects, initiatives, or objectives. In this section, we'll discuss the fundamentals of strategic partnerships and how businesses can leverage them to create value and drive growth.

Drawing on examples from companies like Apple and Nike, who collaborated on the development of the Nike+ iPod sport kit, and Microsoft and Adobe, who partnered to integrate Adobe Creative Cloud with Microsoft Teams, we'll explore the benefits of strategic partnerships, including access to new markets, technologies, and expertise, as well as cost-sharing and risk mitigation. We'll also discuss different types of strategic partnerships, such as joint ventures, alliances, and licensing agreements, and how businesses can identify and evaluate potential partners to ensure alignment with their strategic objectives and values.

15.2 Building Strategic Alliances: Aligning Objectives and Resources

Strategic alliances involve long-term partnerships between organizations that share complementary strengths, capabilities, and resources to achieve common goals. In this section, we'll discuss strategies for building and managing strategic alliances and how businesses can leverage them to drive innovation, market expansion, and competitive advantage.

Drawing on examples from companies like Starbucks and Nestle, who formed a strategic alliance to market and distribute Starbucks coffee products globally, and Toyota and Mazda, who collaborated on the development of electric vehicle technology, we'll explore techniques for building successful alliances, including establishing clear objectives and expectations, aligning incentives and interests, and fostering trust and communication. We'll also discuss the importance of flexibility and adaptability in managing strategic alliances and how businesses can navigate challenges and conflicts to maximize the value of their partnerships.

15.3 Collaborating with Suppliers and Customers: Creating Value Chains

Collaboration with suppliers and customers is essential for optimizing value chains and delivering superior products and services to the market. In this section, we'll discuss strategies for collaborating with suppliers and customers and how businesses can use these relationships to enhance efficiency, innovation, and customer satisfaction.

Drawing on examples from companies like Walmart and Procter & Gamble, who collaborated on supply chain optimization initiatives to reduce costs and improve inventory management, and Apple and its ecosystem of app developers, who collaborate to create innovative and user-friendly applications for Apple devices, we'll explore techniques for collaborating with suppliers and customers, including joint product development, shared data and insights, and strategic sourcing partnerships. We'll also discuss the importance of transparency, communication, and trust in building strong relationships with suppliers and customers and how businesses can create value through collaboration across the entire value chain.

15.4 Partnering with Competitors: Coopetition and Ecosystems

Partnering with competitors, known as coopetition, can provide businesses with access to new markets, technologies, and opportunities while still competing in other areas. In this section, we'll discuss strategies for coopetition and how businesses can navigate the complexities of collaborating with competitors to achieve mutual benefits.

Drawing on examples from industries like technology, where companies like Apple and Google compete in some areas while collaborating in others, and healthcare, where pharmaceutical companies collaborate on drug development while competing in the marketplace, we'll explore techniques for coopetition, including establishing clear boundaries and rules of engagement, focusing on areas of mutual interest and benefit, and leveraging shared platforms and ecosystems to create value. We'll also discuss the importance of trust, transparency, and communication in building successful coopetitive relationships and how businesses can use coopetition to drive innovation, market expansion, and sustainable growth.

15.5 Managing Strategic Partnerships: Best Practices and Pitfalls to Avoid

Managing strategic partnerships requires careful planning, execution, and ongoing management to ensure success and maximize value for all parties involved. In this section, we'll discuss best practices for managing strategic partnerships and common pitfalls to avoid.

Drawing on examples from companies like Amazon and its network of third-party sellers, who collaborate to expand the selection of products available on the Amazon platform, and IBM and its ecosystem of business partners, who collaborate to deliver integrated solutions to customers, we'll explore techniques for managing strategic partnerships, including establishing clear goals and expectations, defining roles and responsibilities, and developing governance structures and performance metrics. We'll also discuss common challenges and pitfalls in managing strategic partnerships, such as conflicts of interest, misaligned incentives, and cultural differences, and how businesses can proactively address these issues to foster successful collaborations and drive business growth.

15.6 Conclusion: Harnessing the Power of Collaboration for Growth

As we conclude this chapter, it's clear that strategic partnerships and collaboration are essential for businesses looking to drive growth, innovation, and competitive advantage in today's interconnected and dynamic business environment. By understanding the principles of strategic partnerships, building strong alliances with suppliers, customers, and competitors, and effectively managing these relationships, businesses can leverage synergies and shared expertise to create value and achieve their strategic objectives.

In the chapters that follow, we'll delve deeper into other aspects of business management, including leadership, organizational culture, and talent management. But for now, take the time to reflect on the insights and strategies presented in this chapter, and begin implementing them in your own business to harness the power of collaboration for growth and success.

Chapter 16: Risk Management: Safeguarding Business Operations and Assets

Risk management is a critical aspect of business management, involving the identification, assessment, and mitigation of risks that could impact the achievement of business objectives. In this chapter, we'll explore the principles of risk management and discuss strategies for safeguarding business operations and assets against potential threats and uncertainties.

16.1 Understanding Risk Management: The Importance of Proactive Planning

Risk management is the process of identifying, assessing, and managing risks to minimize their impact on business operations and objectives. In this section, we'll discuss the fundamentals of risk management and why it's essential for businesses to adopt a proactive approach to identify and mitigate potential risks.

Drawing on examples from companies like Lehman Brothers, Enron, and Volkswagen, who faced significant financial and reputational damage due to inadequate risk management practices, we'll explore the consequences of ineffective risk management and the importance of proactive planning and risk mitigation strategies. We'll also discuss the role of risk management frameworks and methodologies, such as COSO ERM and ISO 31000, in helping businesses identify, assess, and respond to risks effectively.

16.2 Identifying Risks: From Internal to External Threats

Identifying risks involves systematically identifying and evaluating potential threats and uncertainties that could impact business operations and objectives. In this section, we'll discuss techniques for identifying risks, including both internal and external factors that could pose risks to the organization.

Drawing on examples from industries like cybersecurity, supply chain management, and regulatory compliance, we'll explore different types of risks, including operational risks, financial risks, strategic risks, and compliance risks. We'll also discuss the importance of conducting risk assessments, using tools such as risk registers, risk matrices, and scenario analysis, to prioritize risks based on their likelihood and potential impact on the business.

16.3 Assessing Risks: Quantifying Impact and Likelihood

Assessing risks involves quantifying the potential impact and likelihood of risks to prioritize them for mitigation. In this section, we'll discuss techniques for assessing risks and how businesses can use risk assessment methodologies to make informed decisions about risk management strategies.

Drawing on examples from risk assessment practices used by financial institutions, insurance companies, and manufacturing firms, we'll explore techniques for quantifying risk, including qualitative and quantitative approaches. We'll also discuss the importance of considering both the financial and non-financial impacts of risks, as well as the likelihood of occurrence, in assessing risks and developing risk mitigation plans.

16.4 Managing Risks: Mitigation and Response Strategies

Managing risks involves developing and implementing strategies to mitigate their impact and reduce their likelihood of occurrence. In this section, we'll discuss techniques for managing risks and how businesses can use risk mitigation and response strategies to protect their operations and assets.

Drawing on examples from risk management practices used by companies like Johnson & Johnson, who implemented a recall strategy to mitigate the impact of product recalls, and BP, who developed a crisis management plan to respond to the Deepwater Horizon oil spill, we'll explore techniques for managing risks, including risk avoidance, risk reduction, risk transfer, and risk acceptance. We'll also discuss the importance of developing contingency plans and business continuity plans to respond to unexpected events and minimize the impact of risks on business operations.

16.5 Monitoring and Reviewing Risks: Continuous Improvement

Monitoring and reviewing risks is essential for ensuring that risk management strategies remain effective and responsive to changing circumstances. In this section, we'll discuss techniques for monitoring and reviewing risks and how businesses can use risk management metrics and indicators to track the effectiveness of risk management efforts.

Drawing on examples from risk management practices used by companies like General Electric, who implemented a risk dashboard to monitor key risk indicators, and Target, who conducts regular risk assessments to identify emerging risks, we'll explore techniques for monitoring risks, including regular risk reporting, trend analysis, and scenario planning. We'll also discuss the importance of conducting periodic reviews of risk management processes and procedures to identify areas for improvement and drive continuous improvement in risk management practices.

16.6 Conclusion: Building Resilience Through Effective Risk Management

As we conclude this chapter, it's clear that effective risk management is essential for businesses looking to protect their operations and assets against potential threats and uncertainties. By understanding the principles of risk management, identifying and assessing risks proactively, and implementing effective risk mitigation and response strategies, businesses can build resilience and adaptability to navigate the complexities of the business environment and achieve their strategic objectives.

In the chapters that follow, we'll delve deeper into other aspects of business management, including financial management, strategic planning, and leadership. But for now, take the time to reflect on the insights and strategies presented in this chapter, and begin implementing them in your own business to safeguard your operations and assets against potential risks and uncertainties.

Chapter 17: Financial Management: Navigating the Fiscal Landscape for Business Success

Financial management is a cornerstone of business operations, encompassing the planning, organizing, directing, and controlling of financial activities to ensure the efficient and effective use of resources and the achievement of organizational goals. In this chapter, we'll explore the principles of financial management and discuss strategies for navigating the fiscal landscape to drive business success.

17.1 Understanding Financial Management: The Foundation of Business Operations

Financial management involves the strategic management of financial resources to achieve organizational objectives. In this section, we'll discuss the fundamentals of financial management and why it's crucial for businesses to have sound financial management practices in place.

Drawing on examples from companies like Warren Buffett's Berkshire Hathaway and Elon Musk's Tesla, we'll explore the key components of financial management, including financial planning, budgeting, forecasting, and financial analysis. We'll also discuss the role of financial management in supporting decision-making processes, allocating resources effectively, and maximizing shareholder value.

17.2 Financial Planning and Forecasting: Anticipating Future Performance

Financial planning and forecasting are essential for businesses to anticipate future financial performance and make informed decisions about resource allocation and investment strategies. In this section, we'll discuss techniques for financial planning and forecasting and how businesses can use them to navigate the uncertainties of the business environment.

Drawing on examples from companies like Amazon and Walmart, who use sophisticated financial modeling techniques to forecast future sales and earnings, we'll explore techniques for financial planning and forecasting, including budgeting, variance analysis, and scenario planning. We'll also discuss the importance of considering external factors, such as market trends, economic conditions, and regulatory changes, in financial forecasting and how businesses can use financial forecasts to identify opportunities and risks and make proactive adjustments to their business strategies.

17.3 Budgeting and Resource Allocation: Optimizing Financial Resources

Budgeting and resource allocation are essential for businesses to allocate financial resources effectively and ensure that they are used efficiently to achieve organizational goals. In this section, we'll discuss techniques for budgeting and resource allocation and how businesses can use them to optimize their financial resources.

Drawing on examples from companies like Google and Microsoft, who use zero-based budgeting techniques to allocate resources based on strategic priorities, we'll explore techniques for budgeting and resource allocation, including top-down and bottom-up approaches, activity-based costing, and capital budgeting. We'll also discuss the importance of aligning budgeting and resource allocation decisions with strategic objectives and how businesses can use performance metrics and key performance indicators (KPIs) to monitor and evaluate the effectiveness of their budgeting and resource allocation processes.

17.4 Financial Analysis and Performance Measurement: Evaluating Business Performance

Financial analysis and performance measurement are essential for businesses to evaluate their financial performance and make informed decisions about resource allocation and investment strategies. In this section, we'll discuss techniques for financial analysis and performance measurement and how businesses can use them to assess their financial health and identify areas for improvement.

Drawing on examples from companies like Apple and Coca-Cola, who use financial ratios and benchmarks to evaluate their financial performance relative to industry peers, we'll explore techniques for financial analysis and performance measurement, including ratio analysis, trend analysis, and benchmarking. We'll also discuss the importance of using both financial and non-financial metrics to evaluate business performance comprehensively and how businesses can use financial analysis to identify trends, opportunities, and risks and make proactive adjustments to their business strategies.

17.5 Financial Risk Management: Mitigating Financial Uncertainties

Financial risk management involves identifying, assessing, and mitigating financial risks that could impact business operations and objectives. In this section, we'll discuss techniques for financial risk management and how businesses can use them to safeguard their financial health and stability.

Drawing on examples from companies like JPMorgan Chase and Goldman Sachs, who use sophisticated risk management techniques to manage market, credit, and liquidity risks, we'll explore techniques for financial risk management, including hedging, diversification, and insurance. We'll also discuss the importance of stress testing and scenario analysis in assessing the potential impact of financial risks and how businesses can use risk management frameworks and methodologies to develop robust risk management strategies.

17.6 Conclusion: Achieving Fiscal Fitness for Business Success

As we conclude this chapter, it's clear that financial management is essential for businesses looking to achieve fiscal fitness and drive success in today's competitive business environment. By understanding the principles of financial management, implementing sound financial planning and forecasting practices, optimizing budgeting and resource allocation decisions, conducting rigorous financial analysis and performance measurement, and mitigating financial risks effectively, businesses can navigate the fiscal landscape with confidence and achieve their strategic objectives.

In the chapters that follow, we'll delve deeper into other aspects of business management, including strategic planning, marketing, and human resource management. But for now, take the time to reflect on the insights and strategies presented in this chapter, and begin implementing them in your own business to achieve fiscal fitness and drive success in your business endeavors.

Chapter 18: Marketing Strategies: Navigating the Digital Landscape for Business Growth

Marketing strategies are essential for businesses to reach their target audience, build brand awareness, and drive customer engagement and loyalty. In today's digital age, businesses must navigate a complex landscape of online channels and platforms to effectively promote their products and services. In this chapter, we'll explore the principles of marketing strategies and discuss strategies for leveraging digital marketing channels to drive business growth.

18.1 Understanding Marketing Strategies: The Key to Business Success

Marketing strategies are strategic plans developed by businesses to achieve their marketing objectives and drive business growth. In this section, we'll discuss the fundamentals of marketing strategies and why they are essential for businesses to succeed in today's competitive marketplace.

Drawing on examples from companies like Coca-Cola and Nike, who have developed iconic marketing campaigns to build brand loyalty and drive sales, we'll explore the key components of marketing strategies, including market segmentation, targeting, positioning, and the marketing mix (product, price, place, and promotion). We'll also discuss the importance of aligning marketing strategies with business objectives and how businesses can use market research and consumer insights to develop effective marketing strategies that resonate with their target audience.

18.2 Digital Marketing Channels: Reaching Customers in the Digital Age

Digital marketing channels have revolutionized the way businesses reach and engage with their target audience, offering a diverse range of platforms and tools to promote products and services online. In this section, we'll discuss the various digital marketing channels available to businesses and how they can leverage them to drive customer engagement and growth.

Drawing on examples from companies like Amazon and Airbnb, who have leveraged digital marketing channels such as social media, search engine optimization (SEO), and email marketing to reach millions of customers worldwide, we'll explore the different types of digital marketing channels, including owned, earned, and paid media. We'll also discuss the advantages and challenges of each digital marketing channel and how businesses can develop integrated digital marketing strategies that leverage multiple channels to maximize reach and impact.

18.3 Social Media Marketing: Building Brand Awareness and Engagement

Social media marketing has become an integral part of businesses' marketing strategies, offering a powerful platform for building brand awareness, driving customer engagement, and fostering relationships with customers. In this section, we'll discuss strategies for leveraging social media marketing to achieve marketing objectives and drive business growth.

Drawing on examples from companies like Starbucks and Airbnb, who have built strong brand presences on social media platforms such as Facebook, Instagram, and Twitter, we'll explore techniques for social media marketing, including content creation, community management, and influencer partnerships. We'll also discuss the importance of authenticity, transparency, and responsiveness in social media marketing and how businesses can use social media analytics and insights to measure the effectiveness of their social media marketing efforts and make data-driven decisions to optimize performance.

18.4 Content Marketing: Creating Value and Building Trust

Content marketing involves creating and distributing valuable, relevant, and consistent content to attract and retain a clearly defined audience and drive profitable customer action. In this section, we'll discuss strategies for leveraging content marketing to build brand authority, trust, and loyalty among customers.

Drawing on examples from companies like HubSpot and Buffer, who have developed comprehensive content marketing strategies to educate and engage their target audience, we'll explore techniques for content marketing, including blog posts, ebooks, videos, podcasts, and webinars. We'll also discuss the importance of storytelling, thought leadership, and search engine optimization (SEO) in content marketing and how businesses can use content marketing to address the needs and pain points of their target audience and drive customer engagement and conversion.

18.5 Search Engine Optimization (SEO): Driving Organic Traffic and Visibility

Search engine optimization (SEO) is the process of optimizing a website and its content to rank higher in search engine results pages (SERPs) and drive organic traffic to the website. In this section, we'll discuss strategies for leveraging SEO to improve online visibility and attract qualified leads to the website.

Drawing on examples from companies like Moz and SEMrush, who have developed industry-leading SEO tools and resources to help businesses improve their search engine rankings, we'll explore techniques for SEO, including keyword research, on-page optimization, link building, and technical SEO. We'll also discuss the importance of user experience (UX), mobile optimization, and local SEO in SEO strategy and how businesses can use analytics and monitoring tools to track and measure the effectiveness of their SEO efforts and make data-driven decisions to optimize performance.

18.6 Paid Advertising: Driving Targeted Traffic and Conversions

Paid advertising involves paying for ad placements on digital channels to reach a targeted audience and drive traffic and conversions. In this section, we'll discuss strategies for leveraging paid advertising to complement organic marketing efforts and achieve marketing objectives.

Drawing on examples from companies like Google and Facebook, who offer sophisticated advertising platforms that allow businesses to target specific demographics, interests, and behaviors, we'll explore techniques for paid advertising, including pay-per-click (PPC) advertising, display advertising, social media advertising, and native advertising. We'll also discuss the importance of ad targeting, ad creative, and ad optimization in paid advertising campaigns and how businesses can use analytics and tracking tools to measure the ROI of their paid advertising efforts and make data-driven decisions to optimize performance.

18.7 Conclusion: Navigating the Digital Marketing Landscape for Business Success

As we conclude this chapter, it's clear that digital marketing has become an essential component of businesses' marketing strategies, offering a diverse range of channels and tools to reach and engage with customers online. By understanding the principles of digital marketing, leveraging digital marketing channels effectively, and developing integrated digital marketing strategies that align with business objectives, businesses can drive customer engagement, build brand awareness, and achieve sustainable growth in today's digital age.

In the chapters that follow, we'll delve deeper into other aspects of business management, including human resource management, operations management, and strategic planning. But for now, take the time to reflect on the insights and strategies presented in this chapter, and begin implementing them in your own business to navigate the digital marketing landscape and drive success in your marketing endeavors.

Chapter 19: Human Resource Management: Cultivating Talent for Business Success

Human resource management (HRM) is a crucial function within organizations, responsible for managing the people-related aspects of the business to ensure the effective utilization of human capital and the achievement of organizational goals. In this chapter, we'll explore the principles of human resource management and discuss strategies for cultivating talent and fostering a positive workplace culture to drive business success.

19.1 Understanding Human Resource Management: The People Factor in Business

Human resource management involves the strategic management of human capital to achieve organizational objectives. In this section, we'll discuss the fundamentals of human resource management and why it's essential for businesses to invest in their people to drive business success.

Drawing on examples from companies like Google and Netflix, who have developed innovative HR practices to attract, retain, and develop top talent, we'll explore the key components of human resource management, including recruitment and selection, training and development, performance management, compensation and benefits, and employee relations. We'll also discuss the role of HR in supporting organizational goals and strategies and how businesses can use HRM practices to create a competitive advantage in the marketplace.

19.2 Recruitment and Selection: Attracting and Retaining Top Talent

Recruitment and selection are critical processes within HRM, responsible for attracting and retaining top talent to meet the staffing needs of the organization. In this section, we'll discuss strategies for recruitment and selection and how businesses can use them to build a high-performing workforce.

Drawing on examples from companies like LinkedIn and Facebook, who have developed innovative recruitment strategies to attract top talent, we'll explore techniques for recruitment and selection, including job analysis, sourcing, screening, interviewing, and candidate assessment. We'll also discuss the importance of employer branding, candidate experience, and diversity and inclusion in recruitment and selection processes and how businesses can use technology and data analytics to streamline and optimize their recruitment efforts.

19.3 Training and Development: Investing in Employee Growth and Development

Training and development are essential for businesses to ensure that their employees have the skills and knowledge necessary to perform their roles effectively and contribute to organizational success. In this section, we'll discuss strategies for training and development and how businesses can use them to cultivate talent and foster a culture of continuous learning and improvement.

Drawing on examples from companies like Amazon and Microsoft, who offer extensive training and development programs to support employee growth and development, we'll explore techniques for training and development, including on-the-job training, classroom training, e-learning, mentorship, and coaching. We'll also discuss the importance of aligning training and development programs with organizational goals and individual development plans and how businesses can use performance management systems and feedback mechanisms to assess the effectiveness of their training and development efforts and make data-driven decisions to optimize employee performance and development.

19.4 Performance Management: Setting Expectations and Providing Feedback

Performance management involves setting clear performance expectations, providing regular feedback and coaching, and evaluating employee performance to drive accountability and performance improvement. In this section, we'll discuss strategies for performance management and how businesses can use them to optimize employee performance and drive business results.

Drawing on examples from companies like General Electric and Adobe, who have implemented innovative performance management practices to support employee development and goal achievement, we'll explore techniques for performance management, including goal setting, performance reviews, feedback mechanisms, and performance appraisal systems. We'll also discuss the importance of continuous feedback, recognition, and rewards in performance management and how businesses can use performance data and metrics to identify areas for improvement and develop targeted interventions to enhance employee performance and engagement.

19.5 Compensation and Benefits: Rewarding and Motivating Employees

Compensation and benefits play a crucial role in attracting, retaining, and motivating employees to perform at their best. In this section, we'll discuss strategies for compensation and benefits and how businesses can use them to create a competitive advantage in the labor market and drive employee engagement and satisfaction.

Drawing on examples from companies like Google and Salesforce, who offer competitive compensation packages and comprehensive benefits programs to attract and retain top talent, we'll explore techniques for compensation and benefits, including salary benchmarking, incentive programs, health and wellness benefits, and work-life balance initiatives. We'll also discuss the importance of aligning compensation and benefits programs with organizational goals and values and how businesses can use total rewards strategies to create a compelling employee value proposition and differentiate themselves as employers of choice in the marketplace.

19.6 Employee Relations: Fostering a Positive Workplace Culture

Employee relations are critical for creating a positive workplace culture where employees feel valued, respected, and engaged. In this section, we'll discuss strategies for employee relations and how businesses can use them to build trust, collaboration, and mutual respect among employees and foster a culture of inclusivity and belonging.

Drawing on examples from companies like Zappos and Southwest Airlines, who prioritize employee engagement and empowerment in their organizational cultures, we'll explore techniques for employee relations, including communication strategies, conflict resolution mechanisms, and employee engagement initiatives. We'll also discuss the importance of leadership visibility and accountability in employee relations and how businesses can use employee feedback and surveys to assess workplace culture and identify areas for improvement.

19.7 Conclusion: Investing in People for Business Success

As we conclude this chapter, it's clear that human resource management is essential for businesses looking to cultivate talent, foster a positive workplace culture, and drive business success. By understanding the principles of human resource management, implementing effective HRM practices, and prioritizing the development and well-being of their employees, businesses can create a competitive advantage and achieve sustainable growth in today's dynamic business environment.

Chapter 20: Operations Management: Optimizing Efficiency and Effectiveness for Business Excellence

Operations management is the discipline of managing the processes and resources that create and deliver an organization's products and services. It is concerned with optimizing efficiency, effectiveness, and flexibility in the production and delivery of goods and services to meet customer demands and achieve organizational goals. In this chapter, we'll explore the principles of operations management and discuss strategies for optimizing operations to drive business excellence.

20.1 Understanding Operations Management: The Backbone of Business Operations

Operations management plays a crucial role in ensuring the smooth functioning of business operations and delivering value to customers. In this section, we'll discuss the fundamentals of operations management and why it's essential for businesses to focus on optimizing their operations to achieve competitive advantage and business success.

Drawing on examples from companies like Toyota and McDonald's, who have revolutionized their respective industries through innovative operations management practices, we'll explore the key components of operations management, including process design, capacity planning, inventory management, quality control, and supply chain management. We'll also discuss the role of operations management in driving cost reduction, improving productivity, and enhancing customer satisfaction, and how businesses can use operations management principles to achieve operational excellence and sustainable growth.

20.2 Process Design and Improvement: Streamlining Operations for Efficiency

Process design and improvement involve analyzing, designing, and optimizing business processes to achieve efficiency, quality, and flexibility in operations. In this section, we'll discuss strategies for process design and improvement and how businesses can use them to streamline operations and drive performance improvement.

Drawing on examples from companies like Amazon and FedEx, who have developed highly efficient and scalable business processes to meet customer demands and achieve competitive advantage, we'll explore techniques for process design and improvement, including value stream mapping, process reengineering, and lean manufacturing principles. We'll also discuss the importance of aligning process design with business objectives and customer requirements and how businesses can use process metrics and performance indicators to monitor and evaluate process performance and make continuous improvements to their operations.

20.3 Capacity Planning: Balancing Demand and Supply

Capacity planning involves determining the optimal level of resources needed to meet customer demand while maintaining cost efficiency and flexibility in operations. In this section, we'll discuss strategies for capacity planning and how businesses can use them to optimize resource utilization and achieve operational efficiency.

Drawing on examples from companies like Apple and Samsung, who use sophisticated capacity planning models to forecast demand and optimize production capacity, we'll explore techniques for capacity planning, including demand forecasting, capacity analysis, and resource allocation. We'll also discuss the importance of considering factors such as seasonality, market trends, and technological advancements in capacity planning and how businesses can use capacity planning to manage risks, minimize costs, and maximize revenue generation.

20.4 Inventory Management: Balancing Costs and Customer Service

Inventory management involves managing the flow of goods and materials throughout the supply chain to ensure that the right products are available in the right quantities at the right time to meet customer demand while minimizing costs and optimizing cash flow. In this section, we'll discuss strategies for inventory management and how businesses can use them to achieve inventory efficiency and improve customer service.

Drawing on examples from companies like Walmart and Amazon, who have developed sophisticated inventory management systems to optimize inventory levels and reduce stockouts and excess inventory, we'll explore techniques for inventory management, including demand forecasting, inventory optimization, and just-in-time (JIT) inventory systems. We'll also discuss the importance of inventory accuracy, inventory visibility, and supplier collaboration in inventory management and how businesses can use inventory metrics and performance indicators to monitor and evaluate inventory performance and make data-driven decisions to optimize inventory levels and improve customer satisfaction.

20.5 Quality Control: Ensuring Product and Service Excellence

Quality control involves monitoring and controlling the quality of products and services to meet customer expectations and regulatory requirements. In this section, we'll discuss strategies for quality control and how businesses can use them to achieve product and service excellence and build customer trust and loyalty.

Drawing on examples from companies like Toyota and Ford, who have implemented rigorous quality control processes to ensure the reliability and safety of their products, we'll explore techniques for quality control, including statistical process control, total quality management (TQM), and Six Sigma. We'll also discuss the importance of continuous improvement, employee involvement, and customer feedback in quality control processes and how businesses can use quality metrics and performance indicators to monitor and evaluate quality performance and make proactive adjustments to their operations to achieve quality excellence.

20.6 Supply Chain Management: Integrating and Optimizing the Supply Chain

Supply chain management involves managing the flow of goods, services, and information from suppliers to customers to maximize value creation and achieve competitive advantage. In this section, we'll discuss strategies for supply chain management and how businesses can use them to optimize supply chain performance and drive business success.

Drawing on examples from companies like Procter & Gamble and Unilever, who have developed agile and responsive supply chains to adapt to changing market conditions and customer demands, we'll explore techniques for supply chain management, including supplier relationship management, logistics optimization, and demand forecasting. We'll also discuss the importance of collaboration, visibility, and risk management in supply chain management and how businesses can use supply chain analytics and performance metrics to monitor and evaluate supply chain performance and make data-driven decisions to optimize supply chain efficiency and effectiveness.

20.7 Conclusion: Achieving Operational Excellence for Business Success

As we conclude this chapter, it's clear that operations management is essential for businesses looking to achieve operational excellence and drive business success. By understanding the principles of operations management, implementing effective operations management practices, and prioritizing continuous improvement and innovation in operations, businesses can optimize efficiency, effectiveness, and flexibility in their operations to meet customer demands, achieve competitive advantage, and achieve sustainable growth in today's dynamic business environment.

Conclusion: Navigating the Business Landscape with Confidence

In the journey through the pages of "Dollar and Sense: Practical Advice for Business Owners," we have embarked on a comprehensive exploration of the multifaceted world of business management. From strategic planning to financial management, marketing strategies to human resource management, and operations management to supply chain optimization, we have delved deep into the intricacies and complexities of running a successful business in today's dynamic and competitive environment.

As we reflect on the insights and strategies presented throughout this book, it becomes evident that success in business requires a multifaceted approach, blending sound principles with innovative thinking, strategic vision with practical execution, and adaptability with resilience. The business landscape is constantly evolving, shaped by technological advancements, market dynamics, regulatory changes, and shifting consumer preferences. To thrive in this ever-changing landscape, business owners must embrace change, cultivate agility, and continuously seek opportunities for growth and improvement.

Throughout this book, we have drawn inspiration from industry leaders and successful entrepreneurs who have navigated the complexities of the business world with courage, creativity, and determination. From visionary leaders like Steve Jobs, who revolutionized the technology industry with his bold innovations at Apple, to pioneering entrepreneurs like Oprah Winfrey, who built an empire from humble beginnings, we have learned valuable lessons in leadership, innovation, and resilience.

We have also explored the importance of strategic planning in setting a clear direction for the business, identifying opportunities and risks, and aligning resources and capabilities to achieve strategic objectives. Whether it's developing a compelling vision, conducting thorough market research, or formulating actionable strategies, strategic planning provides the roadmap for business success and ensures that every decision and action is guided by a clear purpose and direction.

Financial management has emerged as another critical aspect of business success, encompassing the planning, organizing, directing, and controlling of financial activities to ensure the efficient and effective use of resources and the achievement of organizational goals. From budgeting and forecasting to financial analysis and risk management, effective financial management practices are essential for businesses to navigate the fiscal landscape with confidence and drive sustainable growth.

Marketing strategies have also been explored in depth, highlighting the importance of understanding customer needs and preferences, building brand awareness and loyalty, and leveraging digital marketing channels to reach and engage with target audiences effectively. In today's digital age, businesses must embrace the power of social media, content marketing, search engine optimization, and paid advertising to create meaningful connections with customers and drive business growth.

Human resource management has emerged as a critical factor in business success, emphasizing the importance of recruiting and retaining top talent, providing opportunities for employee growth and development, and fostering a positive workplace culture that values diversity, inclusion, and collaboration. By investing in their people, businesses can build high-performing teams, drive employee engagement and satisfaction, and ultimately, achieve organizational excellence.

Operations management has been highlighted as another key determinant of business success, focusing on optimizing efficiency, effectiveness, and flexibility in the production and delivery of goods and services. From process design and improvement to capacity planning, inventory management, and quality control, effective operations management practices are essential for businesses to meet customer demands, minimize costs, and maximize profitability.

Supply chain management has also been emphasized as a critical component of business success, emphasizing the importance of integrating and optimizing the flow of goods, services, and information from suppliers to customers. By developing agile and responsive supply chains, businesses can adapt to changing market conditions, minimize risks, and enhance customer satisfaction.

As we conclude our journey through "Dollar and Sense: Practical Advice for Business Owners," it's clear that success in business is not a destination but a journey—a journey of learning, growth, and continuous improvement. By embracing the principles and strategies presented in this book, business owners can navigate the complexities of the business landscape with confidence, seize opportunities for growth, and achieve their vision of success.

In the words of Richard Branson, "Business opportunities are like buses, there's always another one coming." As business owners, let us embrace change, seize opportunities, and embark on the journey of entrepreneurship with courage, creativity, and determination. Together, we can navigate the business landscape with confidence, overcome challenges, and achieve our goals of building successful and sustainable businesses that make a positive impact in the world.

Thank you for joining me on this journey. Here's to your success in business and in life.

Acknowledgments

I would like to express my sincere gratitude to all those who have contributed to the creation of this book, "Dollar and Sense: Practical Advice for Business Owners."

First and foremost, I am deeply thankful to my family for their unwavering support and encouragement throughout this journey. Their love, patience, and understanding have been my rock, enabling me to pursue my passion for writing and entrepreneurship.

I extend my heartfelt thanks to the team at [King's Media Consult], whose dedication and expertise have brought this book to life. From editorial and design to marketing and distribution, your hard work and commitment to excellence have been instrumental in making this project a reality.

I am also grateful to the countless individuals and organizations who have inspired and influenced my thinking on business management and entrepreneurship. From industry leaders and successful entrepreneurs to mentors, colleagues, and peers, your insights and perspectives have enriched my understanding of the complexities of business and provided valuable inspiration for this book.

Special thanks to my Mentor, whose guidance and mentorship have been invaluable to me throughout my career. Your wisdom, experience, and support have helped shape my approach to business management and provided valuable guidance and inspiration for this book.

Last but not least, I would like to thank the readers of this book for their interest and support. It is my sincere hope that the insights and strategies presented in these pages will provide valuable guidance and inspiration to business owners and entrepreneurs as they navigate the complexities of the business landscape and pursue their dreams of success.

Thank you.

John G. Stringer

www.ingramcontent.com/pod-product-compliance
Lightning Source LLC
Chambersburg PA
CBHW050101230526
45470CB00004B/1634